Conversations before noon

By: Charlynne Bryan

Conversations before noon

Copyright 2019 © by Charlynne Bryan

This book is copyright under the Berne convention and as such no reproduction of this book should be made without the permission of the author. If you share poems from this book on social media, please credit the author.

Instagram: @mizz_b_ryan
Twitter: @cookieb20

Charlynne Bryan

To Shantel, for always keeping me honest
even when honesty is hard.

Conversations before noon

Poetry has the power to get you thinking, dreaming, talking. One poem can resonate with many people for different reasons and in different ways. Within the pages of this book, are several poems. These poems are conversation starters. These poems are words of life. These poems are my thoughts spilled onto paper. I invite you to explore the poetry in this book and use them to begin your own conversations before noon.

Charlynne Bryan

Fire

Conversations before noon

Charlynne Bryan

Don't leave

Touch my skin

Feel how I burn for you

Run your fingertips along

The inside of my thighs

Feel how I flood for you

Taste the honeydew from

My pot of gold

Feel how I lust for you

Before you go, kiss me again

And know that I long for you

Conversations before noon

My body is a playground
Designed for your pleasure

Charlynne Bryan

No name holds promise

like yours

it is the sweet longing

for an ice lolly on a

hot summer day

Desire

You kissed me
Our tongues danced
A tango at the sunset club
You pushed me up against a wall
Everything stood at attention
You plastered your body against
Mine – skin to skin
Fitted me like a wetsuit after a dive
I panted for you, waited with closed eyes.
You
Teased me with your tongue
Then uttered your goodbyes
My fingers took over where yours left off.

Charlynne Bryan

Longing

I woke up feeling lonely
You were not beside me
But I ask myself, "Why am I missing
something I never had?"
I have always slept alone and
Woken up with nothing but dreams.
You never stayed the night
So why now do I long for your head
On the pillow next to mine?
Why do I yearn for your breath fanning my
cheeks
As I lean into your neck?
Why do I want you in my bed
Till the morning light drenches every corner
of my room?
Maybe I want to chase you out of the
darkness that is my night
Force you into the daylight so I can name you
Maybe I want you in the morning to prove to
myself
That you are more than just dreams.

Wordsmith

I always knew that I was good with words

Everyone told me so

What they didn't tell me however

Was how I could bring men to their knees

With a single sound

Or how I could command attention

By just opening my mouth

They also forgot to mention

That my tongue held the power

To stir up the passions that laid dormant

Deep within and

Make volcanoes erupt

Those things I learnt myself

Charlynne Bryan

Why do I chase your beauty?
It's because you are happiness
And I am starving

Conversations before noon

Skin

This skin is a map

Taking the navigator on a

Journey of sensory

Exploration

Charlynne Bryan

I will wait for you

For as long as it takes

You are worth it

To my new love

I will be difficult at first
Hair-pulling, head-knocking difficult
Hard work.
I will have you dancing around me in circles
And every time you reach out,
I will shrink away.
I will make plans with you
Talk dreams with you
Smile wide with you
Then deny you the pleasures of me
Be patient with me, remember...
I was just broken.

I will be sceptical at first
Nerves-inducing, heart-palpitating sceptical.
You will offer to help me pick up the pieces
and while you do,
I will regard you with suspicion
Trying to figure you out...
When it's your motives I cannot be clear
about
Be patient with me,

Coming through hell has grazed me, bruised
me, cut me deep
And now I must learn to trust myself again
As well as you too
It gon' take time boo boo.

I will be elusive at first
Spine-chilling, mind-numbing elusive
We will dance a slow dance held
Close to each other, my cheek resting against
yours
We will talk about our future while floating
towards the clouds
Then you won't find me.
I would have gone,
I would have run.
As fast as possible, as far as possible away
From your promises.
Be patient with me
I just had my soul ripped out; my spirit
almost taken.

I will be trouble at first
The kind you find only when you go looking for
it

Conversations before noon

I will rub you the wrong way until you bleed
I will take all you have to offer and refuse to
give
I will let you know in no uncertain terms
That I can do without you
That I really do not need you
That I am ok on my own...
Be patient with me
I was just shown the dark side of love and
survived
My mind is not yet really my own

I will be a caution sign at first
But I can assure you...
If you wait on me, are patient with me, love
me
Regardless,
I will be... Worth. The. Wait.

Charlynne Bryan

I talk about you all the time

You need to stop falling into my conversations
It's a bad habit I've noticed you have
suddenly picked up
Things always begin quite innocently and
For the first few minutes you remain at bay
But soon you hijack your way out of my brain
Glide down through my senses and roll off my
tongue
You jump into action like an acrobat in full
swing
Dashing across the platform of my words
swinging
To and fro between my stories
Hanging in the air as you invoke awe and
suspense
At first, you elude me
You play like a whisper on my heart
Then a game of hide and seek starts
With you jumping out on ten
before I know it
You are there again
I smile and acknowledge your presence

Conversations before noon

Wonder if people notice that you're back yet
another time
And I make a mental note to remind you that
You must keep away
But I know it will happen again tomorrow
Because you cannot keep out of my
conversations and
I have come to look forward to you jumping
out as you do

Charlynne Bryan

Him

What inspires you?
For me it's him and those soulful eyes
Eyes so full of soul hmm
They take me – here, there, everywhere
He steps into the room and
I forget my own name, damn this is insane.
Just his presence alone wreaking havoc on my
brain,
Slow rhythm of my pulse racing up - full
speed
And forbidden places, longing. Filling up with
need.
And how I crave him and him alone, what
greed!
Like how he is barely there
A whisper on the air
Seating away from me but still too near
And I feel him
Peel back my senses and crawl beneath my
skin
Play a tune on my heart and ignite a fire
within.

Conversations before noon

Slow burning volcano, lava flow about to
begin.
he does it for me – every time
it's crazy but somewhere deep inside, he's
mine
and though he doesn't know it yet, he will in
time
what excites me? He does.
It's always him. Every time.

Charlynne Bryan

Let me tell you about a man I knew

He knew how to look at me
Like there was fire in my being
and I could light him up.
He would touch me with only his eyes and
ignite flames of passion so strong,
I would become consumed.
Then he would reach out and caress my skin,
Singeing my hesitation with his fingertips.
The contact set me alit and as he would pull
me close
Oh how we would burn.
Embers of passion smouldering through the
night
Kept ablaze by the heat of his kisses alone;
And come morning I would be
reduced to ashes – scorched beyond
recognition.
He. Was always the match needed to begin
the flare.
He. Would build up to a simmer then
disappear.
Me. Once burnt, twice shy.

Conversations before noon

You always had the power to cut me
Deeper than any blade I pressed against my
skin
to chase out the demons I couldn't cope with.
The razor of your eyes held me pinned
To the accusations you did not need to speak.
He is nothing like you
His words are sweet honey dripping onto my
ears
Nourishing my being
His eyes, the healing I need to continue
surviving
His touch, a caress more caring than
I have ever known
Yet each time his soul tries to connect with
mine
I fear that he will become just like you
For you started off loving me too.

His love is refreshing.
A love I have never felt before
That heals my broken heart by gluing the
pieces back together
And kissing the cracks out...
Is it love I feel when he dips his head
between my legs and
unleashes an avalanche?
Or is it love I feel when
He thrusts into me and fills up the
longing in my soul
I shudder under his caress
I tremble when his lips touch mine
I surrender to the king in him
Curve into his arms as my body moulds
perfectly
To his frame
I give in to sensations running through me
On a whisper of his name
The way he loves me is refreshing
But have I confused passion for love?

I love you

I don't know how to say
I love you
Without lacing those words
With regret and pain
It's true love doesn't hurt; people do
But when I become a shadow
Whittled down by the burden of
A misguided idea of love
When you come to me with love in your eyes
No matter how real
I struggle to say
I love you
And know what that really means

Charlynne Bryan

Betrayal

My body betrays me
When I am with you
Screaming things I have no
Courage to say:
You complete me
I am your destined
My heart beats for you
I LOVE you...

Love language

I'm an expert in the language
Of my body...
Yet my hands can never
Make my body talk
The way your fingertips does...

Charlynne Bryan

Water

Conversations before noon

Charlynne Bryan

You told me words are life.

I believed you

Until you used

Your words

To destroy me.

Conversations before noon

You stare into my
    Soul
Searching for
    Eternity...
I close my eyes.

Charlynne Bryan

Countless days spent with you

Leaves me aching for things

I cannot have

Conversations before noon

I am all that I need to be

And if you don't accept me

Then you aren't good for me

Charlynne Bryan

Labels

I am not afraid
of what I call myself
And consequently what
I will become as a
result of those labels
It's what I call you
that scares me.

Conversations before noon

The wait is a ticking time bomb
Always on countdown
Ready to explode
And causing a commotion
When it finally does

Charlynne Bryan

Rubix cube

No one has the patience for them anymore
But it's clear
You are a practised
Guru in the art of patience
As you twist and turn your fingers
Manipulating the cubes in the direction you
Will them to turn
Each twist a beckoning
Causing colours to form
And it's clear you have done this before
Countless hours
Spent mindfully
Assembling
You, the architect of dreams
Them, your canvas
You rest assured that this
Your masterpiece will reveal
Your genius
And it tells your story
How you rose through the ranks
Becoming champion
How you, an inspiration,
A conundrum

Conversations before noon

Were able to form magic with your
Fingertips
All because you were
A patient man.

Charlynne Bryan

Soon

And so
You just keep on
Keeping on
Through every heartbreak
You just keep it steady
One foot in front the other
One step at a time
Soon
Soon I promise
Soon
It won't hurt so much.

Conversations before noon

Have you ever felt yourself breaking?
Sometimes I break in seven languages
All at once
But never in a language my heart
Can comprehend

Charlynne Bryan

Don't love me until you love me

If love is the choice you make
Then choose
To be with me
Unconditionally only
And choose
To be kind enough to walk away
From me when
Loving me is no longer your choice

Lost and found

I tend to lose people
The way I lose keys
For a moment I hold them
In the palm of my hands,
Their importance weighing on my mind
They unlock doors to empty rooms waiting
To be filled with memories
They step in, build a home on the shelves in
my heart
Hinge themselves onto the brick walls
I had used to shield me
Make their nests in the grooves of my soul
And then, like the whispering wind
That bristles the trees on a light spring day,
They're gone
It's no wonder that I choose to lock myself
Behind closed doors and throw the keys away

Charlynne Bryan

His breath is a sweet caress
Brushing against my skin
Turning into the sweetest
Poison I've ever tasted

Conversations before noon

3 course meal

I stand corrected
Hold my mouth shut
As I eat the silence
You served as dessert
This isn't
An easy truth to swallow
By any means
And the undigested remains
Threaten to suffocate
But you have made your choice
And now I must,
Dignity intact
Choose
To walk away
From this once full buffet
Turn my back on
The banquet of dreams once on offer
And starve.

Charlynne Bryan

You sell me the illusion
Of happily ever after
And like a fish mesmerised by
A juicy bait,
I bite.

Conversations before noon

Charlynne Bryan

Earth

Conversations before noon

Charlynne Bryan

On losing you

I have waited for you my whole life.
You came for a short time
And didn't stay at all.
I hope I get to meet you again,
Someday – somewhere

Conversations before noon

Some days twenty-four hours are too much

When pain eats at your soul
And hope evades you
When everything you thought you were living
for
Gets ripped out from right under your feet
When people look at you with pity
Offering a sorry you don't want to hear
Or skirting around you with too much care
You just know
That though you cannot go back and change it
You also cannot fast forward to a time when
It no longer hurts
And you cry, deep tears of sorrow
Wishing for escape
You face the truth of your hurt and know:
Some days twenty-four hours are too much

Charlynne Bryan

Find me

You make a smile shine in my heart
And no matter where I am lost
In heaven or on earth
You will find me
and bring me back
to you.

Conversations before noon

Go away!
Stop talking
Every minute you stay
Is making me remember
That I cannot have you
Even though I really
Really want you.

Charlynne Bryan

Saying sorry is the hardest

We fight like there is no tomorrow
It is easy to blame you for being human
Easy to point my finger in the direction of
your sins
Say they equate you to the devil
Easy to think of how to get back at you
Easy to use my tears to make you feel like
you really are wrong
And my silence to make all that happened
seem louder
It is even easy to kiss and make up
Easy to forget about it
Easy to not mention it
Easy to let sleeping dogs lie
All this time, we go through the motions of
easy
It's saying sorry which is the hardest.

Be bold, be brave

We all have demons we cannot face
sometimes
Scary, ugly, goblin things eating up our insides
You may learn to cope by putting on a smile
Another deal with the devil by going AWOL
for a while
But sometimes our demons cannot be
contained
No chains are strong enough to hold them,
they will not be tamed
they seep out through our eyes and mouth,
reap a raging war
They are just bursting at the seams, to be
contained no more
And we hurt an unsuspecting few, though
perhaps unintentionally
I can only apologise for my demons and say,
'They are not me.'
Those nasty, dirty, ugly things sometimes
corrupt what I see
And then I erupt in a way that was never
meant to be
But it's my demons really, it is not me.

Traces

She left traces of herself everywhere she
went
And sometimes she found them
when she trod the path again
Her smile bounced back to her
from the mouths of familiar strangers
Her heartbeat echoed along the walls of the
art gallery where she met her love
Her tears watered the flowers that now
bloomed in her garden
And became the dew drops that lined their
petals
Her fears clung to the structures at the
adventure park
Her laughter danced on the wind and twirled
to a joke told long ago
And sometimes if you listened hard enough
you could hear her silence
Whispering a prayer for you and your journey
Because she is experience and
She left traces of herself everywhere she
went

Conversations before noon

The truth is a lie

The truth is a lie that he told her to keep her
sweet
And she believed it
She took him on his word when he said it
She knelt in front of him and placed her faith
in it
She decided to stand by his truth and live by
it
But his truth ate slowly at her insides
His actions told an alternative story
From the truth he tried to sell
And she had, by this time already
become a shadow of herself
Because instead of living her truth
she had chosen to live his
And his truth is a lie

Charlynne Bryan

Her lips said I'm ok
But her eyes told another story
And she forgot
That we could look into her soul
When its windows were opened wide
And facing ours

Overtime it gets easier. Never easier but easier.

Your absence stretches over days I can no longer count
And it seems that the memories of you are slowly fading away
Even the love I felt has settled and the dust has
covered it; it no longer chokes me the way it used to
tears no longer come as quickly when your name dances across my memory
it no longer hurts me like before
and though I avoid the places where you were laid to rest
overtime it gets easier
Easier to breathe, easier to live, easier to be
I still dream of the possibilities of you in my arms
Me soothing your worries and easing your pain
You, growing up into my boy. My little boy. My strong boy.
My big boy. My little man.

Charlynne Bryan

You would have been a ray of sunshine, a
bubble of pure light
But though you are not here, and you never
really were
Overtime it gets easier. Never easier but
easier.

Conversations before noon

Running

She learnt
To run away from you while
You were stealing her innocence
With your head thrust between her legs
She learnt
That running did not mean putting
Her feet to the ground and pounding
pavement
Until she was out of your grasp and your
Tongue no longer twirled in places where
Little girls should never be tasted so young
She closed her eyes and escaped
Told herself a lullaby that lulled her to sleep-
like numbness
As you stole her virtue
Instead of crying out into an echo
That no one could hear or even want to
She cried into an abyss
And ran
Into herself
She learnt
That to run only meant having a place to run
to

Charlynne Bryan

And she chose to run
To a place where you could not taste
A place where your assaults held
No meaning
She ran
Into the childhood she wanted
If you had not been around.

Conversations before noon

Every now and then
I think of how you left me
broken
And how the pieces of me
Cannot
Fit back together even if
I tried
Because you were the glue
Holding
My seams together.
But now you are gone
I shatter a little more
Fractures that scatter
Into dust
Not even the wind
can harness
Those specs of me that you
left behind.

Lost together

Let's get lost together
And explore the road less travelled
Down cobbled streets, past towering pine
trees.
Let our internal compass guide us
To places beyond our imagination
Where only dark alleys lead.
Watch the child that lurks just on the other
side of your eye
Jump to the forefront and take charge...
Live in the moment, with the moment, for the
moment.
Live...
Let's get lost together
Where no one has gotten lost before
Let's get lost with each other
And while lost, let's explore
Let's get lost together
Because one thing we know is true
Life should be an adventure
But it's only that when I am lost with you.

Conversations before noon

Capture each moment
And really live it
Taste the flavour of experiences
As they flow around your tongue.
Savour every single bite.

People will disappoint you when
They don't do things your way.
Your anger may bubble over
Threaten to overflow because
You cannot just go with the flow...
But you must untie those strings
Tell yourself to let go
Relinquish all control and allow yourself
To be free.
Let. People. Make. Their. Choices.
Just like you, they need to walk their own
path,
Make their own mistakes, be their own
person.
So, focus on mastering only you
Centre yourself and breathe the freedom in
As you give people their liberation
For it is only in setting people free that
You can be free yourself.

Conversations before noon

This woman in the mirror
Is your friend
Her reflection seeks to remind you
Of your beauty
You fixate on her faults
The flaws they multiply as you stare
Questions revolve around in your mind
Why can't I be prettier? Why can't I be
thinner, curvier?
Why can't I be paler? Darker?
Is that a dimple in my thigh?
Is this another wrinkle? Where did this grey
hair come from?
And you continue, not noticing her shrinking
into herself
She is begging you to stop and look into her
eyes
Her plea is silent, but her echo screams
loudly:
'Love me, appreciate me, be happy with me!'
When will you decide that enough is enough?
When will she gain your approval?
You should start today. Now.
Not after the next few pounds or the next
hair dye

Reach out and touch her. Connect her hands to yours
Connect your hands to hers. Link your souls and
Show her that you know the truth,
You are good enough, just as you are!

Conversations before noon

Game on

Get off your seat it's time for a change
The dice has been cast now you need to play
the game
Stop waiting to be told when it's your turn to
make a move
You are already on the board, go on, get into
the groove
The race has started and it's a race you must
run
Ready, steady, move. Go Go Go … Game on!

Charlynne Bryan

Peace

Peace
Flows like water
Washes the soul in
Its basin of crystal clear,
Cleanses.
The raging storm in your heart
Slows down –
Then stops.
Peace soothes like ointment
Healing scars of hunger for more
Soothing bruises of anger
Bandaging up the pain that
Years of accepting just couldn't
Erase.
Peace heals like medicine,
Is medicine, administered
Dose by dose
Until tranquillity flows.
Peace is life
Its ebb and flow
Purifying, renewing.
It dispels doubt and rebuilds
A repertoire of trust.

Conversations before noon

Peace is everything.
Peace is everything.
Peace is.

Charlynne Bryan

I am a butterfly
Bursting out of its cocoon
I am a goddess
Daughter of the sun, stars and moon
I am beauty
I am life and mystery
I am the seasons
All bounded in simple complexity
I am enchantment,
Magic, poetry
I am a beacon of joy
And most importantly
I am me.

Simply heroic

True colours shown
Pure evil at one end
All light at the other...
Just a flip of the coin
Decides which is seen
Yet both parts belong
Seamlessly in this one being.

Charlynne Bryan

Gravitational pull

Our hearts decided we were friends
Before our mind got the message.
We were gravitating toward each other
Right from the beginning of time
And when the lights finally turned
On upstairs we realised that it had
Always been our destiny.

Conversations before noon

Hidden behind the paint

The makeup she wore
was more than just a paste
to cover her years of scars.
It made her face the canvas
She painted on every morning
Until it became art.

Charlynne Bryan

Makeup

I wonder if she knows that she is beautiful
beneath the liquid foundation.
I wonder if she realises that her face is
the building block of perfection.
That under the shimmer of her highlighter
she is the sparkle that illuminates a nation.
I wonder if she believes that her lips should
stick to the truth like the lipstick she glides
on every morning so she could achieve
#perfectpout
I wonder if they are kind words for herself,
those
that rushes out of her mouth.
I wonder if I told her, to her face, how
beautiful
she was, if she would think that
I was talking about her mask...

Conversations before noon

I cry sometimes
When my soul needs a washing
And the smudges of hurt have
Become stuck to the surface
Of everything I am
I allow the water to flow
And ease into the crevices
I cannot reach myself
And clean me
From the inside out
From the outside in.

Charlynne Bryan

Repair kit

I give pieces of myself
Even when others do not
Request it, deserve it
Until I realise that I
Am broken beyond repair.
For while fixing others with
Those fragments of myself,
No one was fixing me.

Power of love

I Love you
These three words are poison
Causing my tongue to rot
Each time they drip from my mouth,
I die a slow death
They rip out my insides and offer them
 to you on a plate
while I look on petrified
They put the power in your hands and
strip me bare
While I wait for you to decide my fate.

Charlynne Bryan

Wait for me
Were never words you heeded when I said
them
They always fell on deaf ears
And I would make up excuses for why
I was the one chasing you through the maze
Of emotions you always seemed to escape
I didn't want to see that
I had given you parts of me you should have
never had
And you were never meant for me in the first
place

Conversations before noon

Charlynne Bryan

Air

Conversations before noon

Charlynne Bryan

Realising truth

You belong to the world
Before you belong to me
And nothing will change that
Not the words I say to you
In the middle of the night
When you need a lullaby
Nor the longing in my chest
Which squeezes the tears from my eyes
You belong to them before
You belong to me
Because that's the choice you made.

Ignorance is bliss

I knew before I knew
That I knew
What I knew
But I chose
Not to know
Because I didn't want to.

Charlynne Bryan

We are one

Alone. I have been that way since
I was born
Then you came along
I fight you at every opportunity
Deny how you make me feel
What you mean to me
But before long
I learn to recognise your essence
For what it is
You are my balance
The ying to my yang. We are
Two halves, separated centuries ago
But now, together again,
We are one.

Conversations before noon

Never settle
    For anything.
Not the dust
    After hell has been raised,
Nor the surrender
    Before the storm has begun.

Charlynne Bryan

Grandma

When fear grips my body
I remember hugging you
Through a thunderstorm
And it is then I know that everything
Is going to be ok.

Conversations before noon

Your time will come
When you least expect it.
It will jump out at you and
Shout, "I am here!"
Stop searching for it.
In the meantime, learn
And grow where you are
Take care of you in this
Space
Make this moment your
Priority; the one that counts
So when your time comes
You will embrace it
With no regrets.

Charlynne Bryan

The sky is the platform
To build upon the dreams
That touched your pillows
The nights when all you had
Left was hope.

Conversations before noon

One step at a time
Isn't always enough when
Each step is loaded with promises
That were broken by someone else.

Charlynne Bryan

Be that as it
May
I will not allow
You to steal
My joy again.

Conversations before noon

Here is the door,
Walk through it.
Don't be afraid of
What's waiting on the
Other side. Just
Know, if it's open
It's meant for you.

Charlynne Bryan

Is this the beginning of the end
Or the end of the beginning?
Am I just kidding myself?
Or are we in the running
For being an example of what
Goals could be
Or are we just frontin' in places where
Others can see?

Conversations before noon

Honesty is the best policy
And I am a believer in the truth, honestly
But every now and then
We are allowed to have
Our secrets
Aren't we?

If you have made it this far
I want to thank you...
For sharing my journey
For accepting my perspective
For allowing me to have my say
You have given me the chance, to be me
And because of this
I am filled with nothing but gratitude for you.

Love and light

Charlynne

Printed in Great Britain
by Amazon

41708029R00057